PIANO SOLO

TOP CHRISTIAN DOWNLOADS

MW00669154

ISBN 978-1-4803-7114-9

HAL•LEONARD®
CORPORATION
7777 W. BLUEMOUND RD. P.O. BOX 13819 MILWAUKEE, WI 53213

Visit Hal Leonard Online at
www.halleonard.com

AMAZING GRACE
(My Chains Are Gone)

Words by JOHN NEWTON
Traditional American Melody
Additional Words and Music by CHRIS TOMLIN
and LOUIE GIGLIO

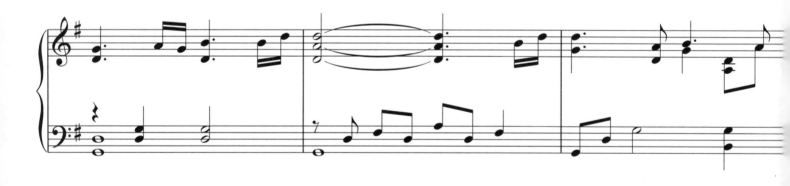

BLESSINGS

Words and Music by
LAURA MIXON STORY

Moderately slow, in 2

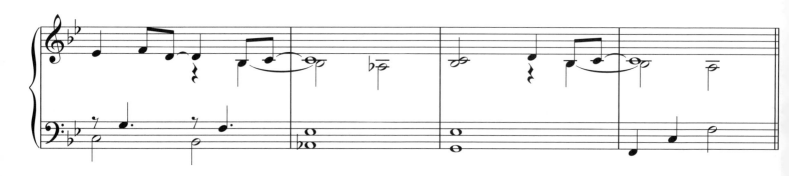

FOREVER REIGN

Words and Music by REUBEN MORGAN
and JASON INGRAM

11-15-15

IN CHRIST ALONE

Words and Music by KEITH GETTY
and STUART TOWNEND

GLORIOUS DAY
(Living He Loved Me)

Words and Music by MARK HALL
and MICHAEL BLEAKER

Moderate Ballad

HOW GREAT IS OUR GOD

Words and Music by CHRIS TOMLIN,
JESSE REEVES and ED CASH

With praise

HOW HE LOVES

Words and Music by
JOHN MARK McMILLAN

Slowly, in 2

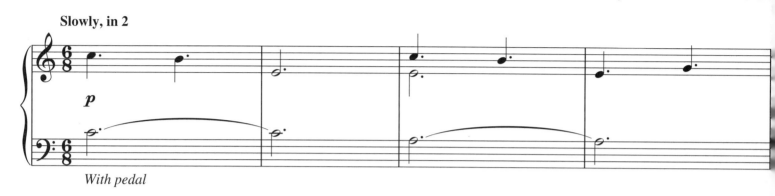

With pedal

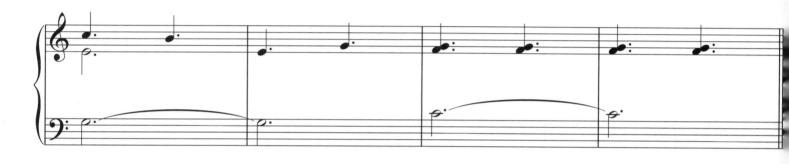

Bring out melody

I CAN ONLY IMAGINE

Words and Music by
BART MILLARD

Reflectively

mp

With pedal

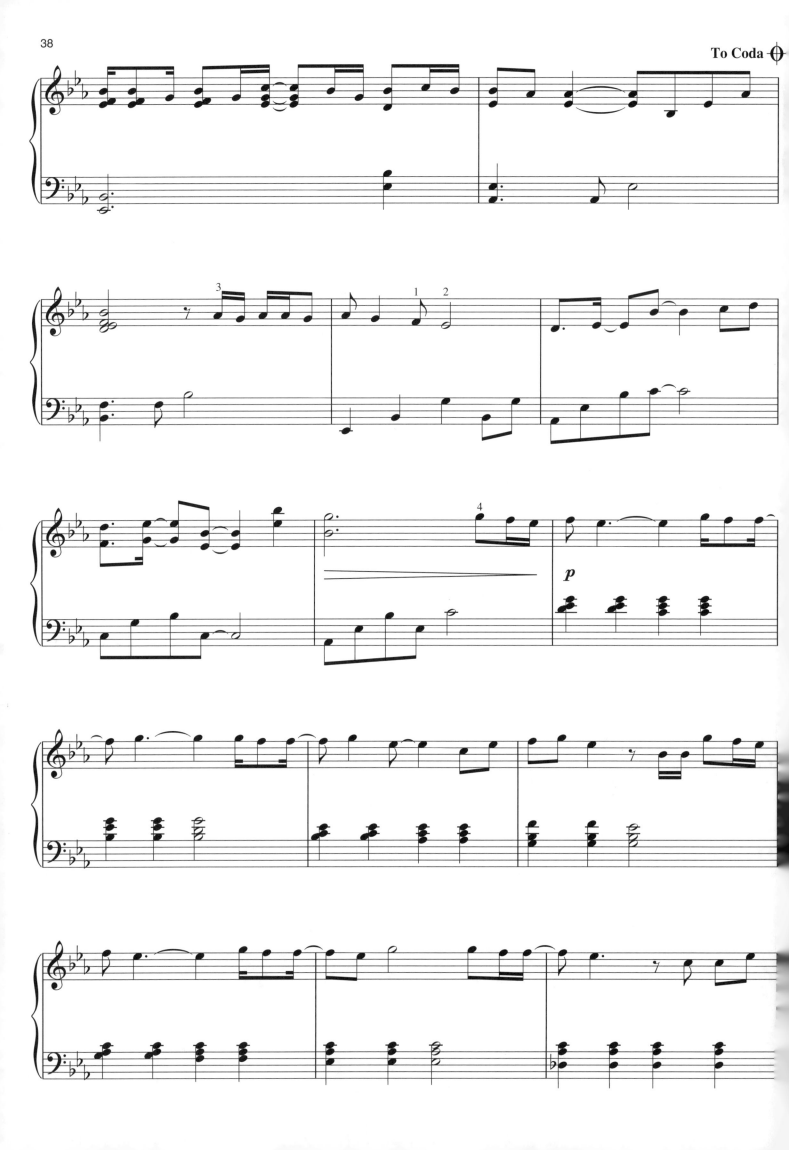

D.S. al Coda

CODA

cresc.

f

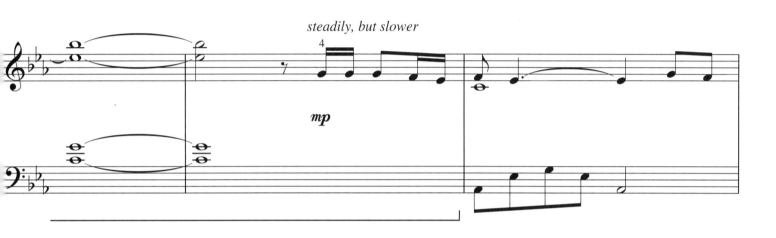

steadily, but slower

I WILL RISE

Words and Music by CHRIS TOMLIN
JESSE REEVES, LOUIE GIGLIO
and MATT MAHER

To Coda ⊕

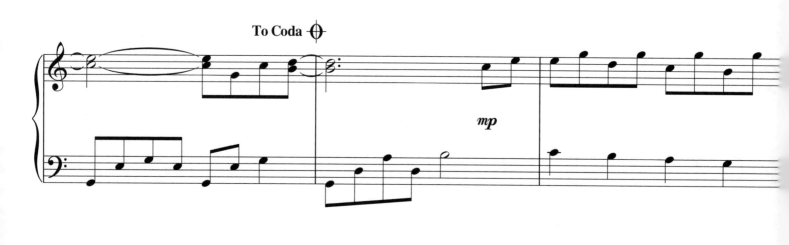

mp

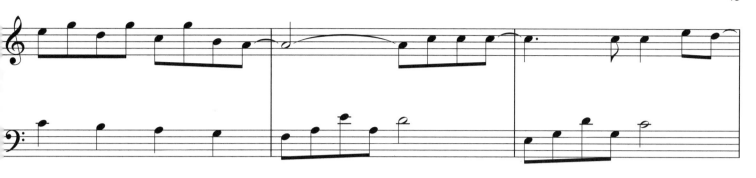

D.S. al Coda

LORD, I NEED YOU

Words and Music by JESSE REEVES,
KRISTIAN STANFILL, MATT MAHER,
CHRISTY NOCKELS and DANIEL CARSON

Moderate Ballad

With pedal

INDESCRIBABLE

Words and Music by LAURA STORY
and JESSE REEVES

Joyfully, in 2

MIGHTY TO SAVE

Words and Music by BEN FIELDING
and REUBEN MORGAN

With praise

MY SAVIOR MY GOD

Words and Music by
AARON SHUST

Moderately

OCEANS
(Where Feet May Fail)

Words and Music by JOEL HOUSTON,
MATT CROCKER and SALOMON LIGHTHELM

OVERCOME

Words and Music by
JON EGAN

Slowly, in 2

REVELATION SONG

Words and Music by
JENNIE LEE RIDDLE

Moderately slow

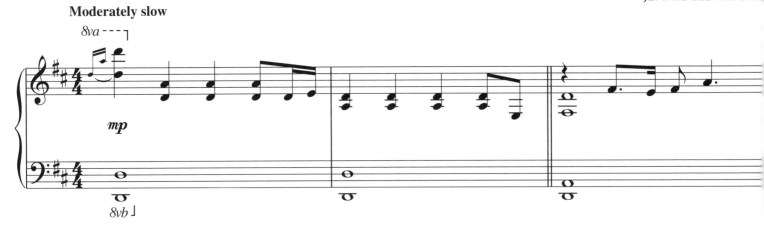

THE STAND

Words and Music by
JOEL HOUSTON

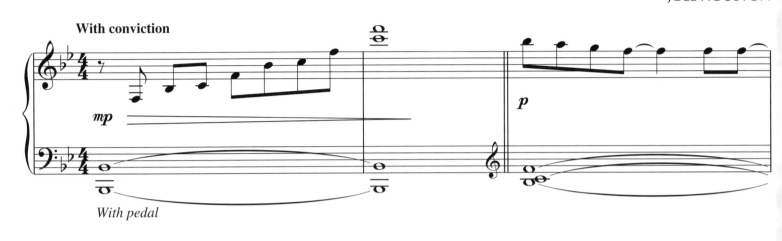

PRAISE YOU IN THIS STORM

Words and Music by MARK HALL
and BERNIE HERMS

10,000 REASONS
(Bless the Lord)

Words and Music by JONAS MYRIN
and MATT REDMAN

Moderate Ballad

WORD OF GOD SPEAK

Words and Music by BART MILLARD
and PETE KIPLEY

Prayerfully, with reverence

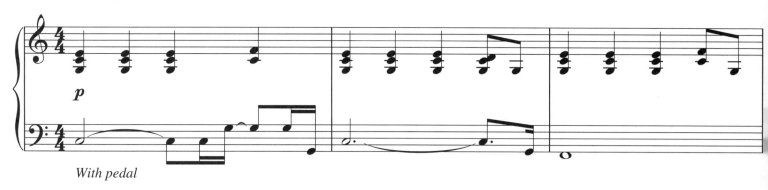

With pedal

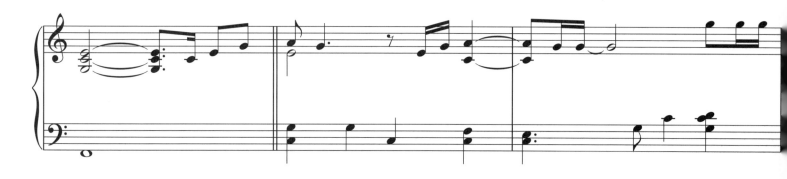

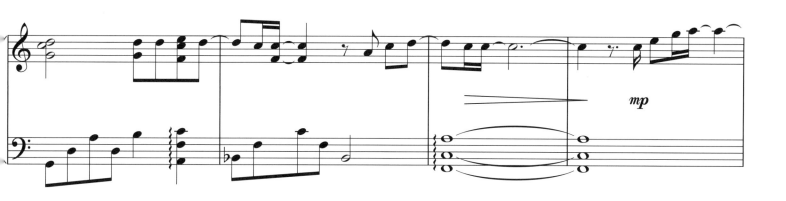

YOUR GRACE IS ENOUGH

Words and Music by
MATT MAHER

To Coda ⊕

8vb